QUAKER QUICKS

Quakers Do What! Why?

QUAKER QUICKS

Quakers Do What! Why?

Rhiannon Grant

CHRISTIAN ALTERNATIVE
BOOKS

Winchester, UK
Washington, USA

JOHN HUNT PUBLISHING

First published by Christian Alternative Books, 2020
Christian Alternative Books is an imprint of John Hunt Publishing Ltd.,
No. 3 East St., Alresford, Hampshire SO24 9EE, UK
office@jhpbooks.com
www.johnhuntpublishing.com
www.christian-alternative.com

For distributor details and how to order please visit the 'Ordering' section on our website.

Text copyright: Rhiannon Grant 2019

ISBN: 978 1 78904 405 8
978 1 78904 406 5 (ebook)
Library of Congress Control Number: 2019948315

A CIP catalogue record for this book is available from the British Library.

Design: Stuart Davies

UK: Printed and bound by CPI Group (UK) Ltd, Croydon, CR0 4YY
US: Printed and bound by Thomson-Shore, 7300 West Joy Road, Dexter, MI 48130

We operate a distinctive and ethical publishing philosophy in all areas of our business, from our global network of authors to production and worldwide distribution.

Contents

Other books by Rhiannon Grant

British Quakers and Religious Language, Brill, 2018, ISBN
9789004378
Telling the Truth about God (Quaker Quicks series), John Hunt
Publishing, ISBN 1789040817

Piangfan Angela Naksukpaiboon: I wish you a future full of good questions.

Acknowledgements

I owe particular thanks to Sophie Bevan and Katie Breslin who gave valuable feedback on a draft of this book. I have also been supported in writing this by Jennifer Kavanagh, colleagues at Woodbrooke, my family, the members of all the Quaker meetings I have attended, and all those who participate in workshops with me. I would like to highlight the contributions of two groups: firstly, attendees at 'Working with Friends' courses, where people who are newly employed by Quaker organisations come together to think through what it means to work for Quakers, whether or not they are Quakers themselves, and secondly, the Leeds Quaker-Jewish Dialogue Group, where I encountered many excellent questions during my brief involvement. Finally, many thanks to everyone who has read my 'I'm a Quaker, ask me why' badge and especially to those who have gone ahead and asked me something.

Introduction

In this book, I'm going to describe and try to explain some of the ways in which Quakers do things differently from other groups. If you've picked this book up because you already had a specific question, you might like to skip to the relevant chapter – but if you are interested in Quakers generally, this introductory chapter gives some more background. It will dispel a few common myths about Quakers, describe the diversity within Quakers, give a whistle-stop tour of some common Quaker terms and references, and tell you a little bit about who I am and why I wrote this book.

Originally a group who broke away from the church during the Civil War in England, Quakers have developed in several directions. Some branches gradually became more like other Protestant groups. Other branches – the ones I will be mainly discussing in this book – moved further away from other churches and towards being either a distinct religion or related to other modern spirituality movements, depending how you look at it. For almost everything, if it can be said about one group of Quakers, there are some others for whom it isn't true. In the first chapter of this book, I talk about a well-known and distinctive Quaker practice, the use of silence in worship – but not every branch of the Quaker family uses silence extensively, or in the same way. In textbooks for teenagers doing religious studies, Quakers often get a few sentences on the page about Christianity and pacifism – and yet research has shown that significant numbers of British Quakers did join the armed forces during the world wars, and around the world Quakers interpret pacifism in different ways.

I do feel comfortable making one generalisation, though. Of all the Quakers in all the world, none of them have anything more to do with oats than anyone else. The Quaker Oats brand is widely recognised, but (unlike other well-known brands which do have a Quaker history, including Cadbury's, Fry's, Rowntree's, Clark's, Barclay's bank, Lloyd's bank, Duane Morris, and Johns Hopkins university) Quaker Oats have no actual Quakers in their history. There are of course many Quakers who like to eat oats. Personally, I like a bowl of porridge on a cold morning – but it has nothing to do with my being a Quaker.

Perhaps I could risk another generalisation, which is that if you ask three Quakers a question you will get at least four answers. That applies even for Quakers who are in the same meeting or church community, because individuals can worship together without agreeing about other things. Quakers are hardly unique in this (I've been told the same thing about members of several other religious communities) but it's worth noting, especially at the start of a book which aims to answer some common questions about Quakers. On the one hand, I'll do my best. I'll point out different possibilities where there are significantly different schools of thought or practice among Quakers. On the other hand, I only have so many words in which to try and please all of the people all of the time – so there will be Quakers who disagree with some of the things I say here. If that's you or someone you know, rest assured that I have no intention of saying that the views represented here are right, or true Quakerism, or better than options not mentioned.

What is included? I've aimed to provide answers to common questions about Quakers, Quaker practice, and how the Quaker community works. A kind of 'Rough Guide to Quakerism', this book tries to help people who are not Quakers get a hang of how Quakers work, and perhaps also be useful for people who are new Quakers, or exploring Quakerism, and need to get their bearings. Here are five top Quaker things to know before we go any further.

1. 'God' means many things. What do you think of when

you hear the word 'God'? Whatever it is, I think it's almost certain that there are some people in the world who both believe in a kind of God AND don't believe in the thing you thought of. I estimate there's an eighty per cent chance that one of them is a Quaker. Quakers sometimes expand the word God with a list of terms to be treated as synonyms: the Light, the Spirit, the Divine, the Mystery, the Ground of our Being, our Parent, the Christ Within, our Teacher, the Buddha, our Beloved, Energy, the Force... Okay, the last one is mostly a joke, but all the others I have really seen or heard Quakers using. In this book, I'll use some of those terms when it seems appropriate, but I'll also often just say 'God'. Don't feel you have to imagine an old man on a cloud: the God Quakers know is timeless but present, infinite and right here with us; is not a man or a woman but has all genders and none (you'll see I repeat 'God' rather than use any pronouns); may or may not be a person or a thing or a story; and is not particularly 'up there' but more often deep down within.

2. **The word 'meeting' has at least three uses.** Firstly, a meeting can be an ordinary meeting, a get-together for whatever purpose: people meet for a committee meeting, or for a Quaker service, a meeting for worship. Secondly, extending from the idea of a meeting for worship, a meeting can be the community, the group of people who regularly come to worship together. Thirdly, extending that even further, a meeting can be a group of Quaker communities who have agreed to work together and have an annual meeting (first sense) to make decisions. This is usually called a Yearly Meeting. Confused? Understandable. Try comparing these uses of the word 'meeting' to the ways we use the word 'church', which can be a building, a local community, or a worldwide community. It might also be helpful to have examples of

all three uses, like this: I go to meeting for worship most weeks. My local meeting for worship is held by Bournville Quaker Meeting (at Bournville meeting house). It's part of Central England Area Meeting and Britain Yearly Meeting. If the word 'meeting' has stopped looking like a real word, be reassured that happens to me sometimes. In this book, I'll try and be clear about which kind of meeting is meant.

3. **You can be a Friend without being my friend.** The formal name for Quakers is the Religious Society of Friends, sometimes shortened to the Society of Friends or just Friends. It can also be used in other phrases, like Friends Church. This gives a lovely image (we're all Friends!) but can be confusing especially in speech. Is 'my friend Rachel' a personal friend of mine or a Quaker? Both, as it happens. In this book I mainly use the word Quaker, thereby avoiding this confusion, but in writing it is possible to distinguish a capital-F Friend, a Quaker, from a small-f friend, a personal friend, from a F/friend, someone who is both.

4. **George Fox founded Quakerism. Pretty much.** I don't talk very much about history in this book. I'll mention it only when I really think it helps to explain why Quakers do what they do. That said, here are a few key historical facts which will help you fit Quakers into their wider context. In 1652, George Fox (claimed later that he) climbed a big hill in the north of England called Pendle Hill, and had a vision in which God showed him many people who could be gathered together. He'd already been having messages from God, and other people were looking for new religious guidance at a time when living in Britain was tumultuous, unpredictable, sometimes violent, and politics was bound up with interpretations of Christianity. People joined Fox: Elizabeth Hooten is reckoned as his first convert, Richard Farnsworth was already travelling with him at

the time of the Pendle Hill incident, and Margaret Fell was convinced soon after and would come to ground the movement through hospitality and letter writing. Within a generation, Quakers had gained significant numbers of converts, published lots of argumentative pamphlets, had their meetings outlawed, spread around Europe and into America, fallen out among themselves (and sometimes made up again), and generally made their mark. Almost every Quaker who wants to prove that the thing they do or want to do is good Quakerism looks to this first generation for a precedent. Unprogrammed worship, careful but unorthodox reading of the Bible, not using violence, and rejecting anything seen as an 'empty ritual' are all open to this kind of justification.

5. **Quakers will surprise you.** As I already said, Quakers around the world are very diverse. Even within a local Quaker meeting, there are usually a lot of differences: different ideas about God, different things people do during the unprogrammed worship, different priorities in life, different backgrounds and experiences, and so on. In this book I make generalisations about Quakers, always trying to be clear when there are common or well-known exceptions, but whatever I say there will always be a Quaker who is different. If you're getting to know Quakers, be ready to ask questions and ready to be surprised. There's probably a Quaker out there right now trying to be as boring and predictable as possible in order to prove this generalisation wrong as well.

Finally, who am I? I grew up in a Quaker family, and went to state school, where I was often the only Quaker and learned to answer questions about Quakerism from a young age. Fascinated by religion, my own and other people's, I studied Philosophy and Theology at university before researching how Quakers talk about God for my PhD. (You can read about the results of that work in my previous book in this series, *Telling the Truth about God*, 2019.) I now work at Woodbrooke, the only Quaker study centre in Europe, where I meet Quakers from around the world and help to facilitate discussions about Quaker practice, beliefs, and communities. I wanted to write this book because I think Quakers are interesting, sometimes amazing, sometimes horrifying, and potentially have a lot to share with the world – but can be very shy. I hope this book helps you understand Quakers better.

At the end of each chapter, I'll include some suggestions about where you can find out more. This isn't the first time someone has produced an introduction to Quakers, although the structure around practical questions gives this book a different approach. To try a different approach, you could look for:

- a book – try Geoffrey Durham, *Being a Quaker: A Guide for Newcomers* (2013, Quaker Quest) for an internal view, or Pink Dandelion *The Quakers: A Very Short Introduction* (2008, Oxford University Press) for a more sociological perspective
- a website – lots of Quaker groups have introductory pages, such as this one by Micah Bales: http://www.quakermaps.com/info
- an audio resource – as well as many podcasts, there are lectures and similar recordings, like this series by Pink Dandelion: https://www.woodbrooke.org.uk/resource-category/a-short-introduction-to-quakerism/
- a video – for example, one of these short videos from QuakerSpeak: http://quakerspeak.com/basics/
- free resources – sent out by some Quaker communities, like these from Britain Yearly Meeting: http://quaker.org.uk/about-quakers/order-a-free-information-pack

Wait – Quakers still exist?

Yes. I understand why people ask this – if you've come across some Quakers in history but never met a living one, it would be an easy mistake to make.

You might have heard of Quakers in the context of British history and especially the Civil War and the Commonwealth, since that's about the time they started. You might have heard of Quakers when talking about the founding of America – Pennsylvania was named after William Penn, a Quaker, and Quakers found both religious freedom and persecution when they had crossed the Atlantic. Mary Dyer, a Quaker, was martyred in Boston, Massachusetts. You might have heard of Quakers in the context of big business, like railways or chocolate – in Bournville, where I live in the south of Birmingham, UK, people often know that the Cadburys were Quakers but only know that means that they didn't drink alcohol.

You might also have heard of other groups who are a bit like Quakers, and have them mixed up. For example, lots of people have heard of the Shakers, famous for the simple designs of furniture and practising celibacy so strictly they have to adopt children. The Shaker community has some things in common with the Quakers, including valuing simplicity and allowing both men and women to take leadership roles, but the Shaker movement is a little bit younger and will probably die out first – in 2017 there were just two Shakers left. In the same year there were estimated to be about 378,000 Quakers.

Another group who get mixed up with the Quakers are the Amish. Again, Quakers have some things in common with the Amish but different roots. The Amish came from continental Europe rather than Britain and are much stricter about keeping themselves separate from the other communities who surround them. For example, the Amish generally don't pay taxes or accept state benefits, while Quakers generally do pay taxes (except when withholding money from the state as a protest), and would accept any state benefits they were entitled to. Many Amish people also refrain from using some types of modern technology – the details vary between Amish communities – but Quakers have no principle against technology. The Quaker tradition does have an emphasis on simplicity or keeping things plain but modern interpretations of this are as likely to come out at 'buy one very good quality computer which will last for years' or 'use a hybrid car which is better for the environment' as 'don't buy a car' or 'stick to a landline telephone rather than getting a smartphone'.

There are other groups, especially other Peace Churches, who are similar to Quakers in some ways. If you start looking into this you might encounter terms like 'anabaptist' (practising adult, believer's baptism rather than offering this ritual to children – see 'Why don't Quakers do things other churches do, like baptism and the eucharist?' for a Quaker take on this), or 'Mennonites' (members of churches inspired by Menno Simons (1496–1561)). Quakers aren't anabaptists or Mennonites, but do have a lot in common with these groups, especially other faith communities who are pacifist.

Want to find out more?

- To check there are really Quakers out there today, you could explore the Friends World Committee for Consultation website or use an Internet search to find your nearest group: http://fwcc.world/
- To learn about the differences between the Quakers and the Amish, watch this video from QuakerSpeak: http://quakerspeak.com/differences-between-quakers-and-amish/
- To get an overview of Quaker history, check out this timeline of key events: https://www.quaker.org.uk/

history-of-quakers

- To learn more about Quaker history, you could join a free online course about the beginnings of Quakerism: https://www.futurelearn.com/courses/quakers
- Or take it even further with the Friends Historical Association: http://www.quakerhistory.org/

Why do Quakers worship in silence? What is Quaker worship like?

Worshipping in silence is a big, unusual, thing about Quakers, and if you've never experienced it, it can be hard to imagine. It can be daunting: how do you sit in silence for that long? It can be stressful: what if you start thinking about something distressing, and you can't stop because there are no distractions? It can be puzzling: why would you want to do that anyway?

It's even more confusing when you realise that not all Quakers do it the same way. Some traditions within Quakerism have what we might call programmed meetings, which include hymn singing, Bible readings, and other elements which would be familiar in other Protestant churches. Even within the so-called 'unprogrammed' tradition, where open or silent worship is the normal way to do things, Quakers sometimes hold 'semi-programmed' worship – some pre-planned and some open, in all sorts of combinations, sometimes for a special occasion and sometimes to make it more accessible or inclusive (to help children participate as well as adults, for example). In this book, which is very short, I'm only going to explore the unprogrammed tradition of Quaker worship.

I'd like to start by describing a real unprogrammed Quaker meeting for worship, in some detail. In the course of my description, I hope you'll see that although silence is important, there's more to Quaker worship than just sitting in silence. Once we've got that description as a common ground, I'll move on to talk about *why* things in Quaker worship are as they are.

It's a Sunday morning, about twenty-five minutes past ten, and I arrive at the Quaker meeting house. I've walked, but as I come through the gate, one Quaker passes me in his car and shortly behind me there's someone in her electric mobility scooter. At the door to the meeting house, someone shakes my hand and says hello. If I visit a meeting where people don't know me, the person on the door also usually asks whether I've been to a Quaker meeting before. Inside, there's a hallway where I can catch my breath, put my umbrella down, and maybe chat for a few minutes, before entering the meeting room.

In the meeting room itself, chairs are set out in a circle. There's a table in the middle with some books, a jug of water, a loop-system microphone, and a vase of flowers, but otherwise the room is mostly plain. When the sun shines, the big windows let in light and white walls reflect it. This was a purpose-built meeting house and one wall has a biblical quotation: God is spirit and they that worship Him must worship Him in spirit and in truth. I choose a chair – picking one with arms because that helps me to be comfortable – and sit down. I move the copy of a little book with a red cover, *Advices & Queries*, which has been put on some of the seats, hang my coat over the back of my chair, and get comfortable. Sometimes I might pick up something to read for a few minutes, but lately I've been wanting that less often.

I sit. Other people come in. We all sit (or maybe one person stands against the wall or lies on the floor), and wait. We listen. I'm a thinking sort of person, and so I'm thinking about stuff that's happened recently, or noticing who's at meeting, or admiring the room or the flowers or the carpet. Today I keep my eyes open but it's also common to close them. Some people actively resist thought, while I find that just makes me feel guilty – so I let my thoughts run and see what they lead to: even the smallest thing, the classic 'what shall I have for lunch?' or similar, can lead to something bigger or deeper: the Last Supper, foodbanks, hospitality as a religious duty.

Someone stands. He speaks briefly about an experience he had recently, in another Quaker meeting as it happens, and the effect it had on him. He tells the story without trying to draw any particular conclusion from it although it was clearly moving. When he sits down, the silence seems deeper. I felt that I could relate to his experience and find myself remembering comparable times in my life. On this occasion, nobody else speaks.

After an hour – marked in our case by a large public clock which is clearly audible in the meeting house – two predetermined people shake hands to end the meeting. The rest of us copy, shaking hands with the two or three people closest to us. One person has come prepared with some notices, and shares information about upcoming events, gaps in the rota for greeting people at the door, and work the meeting supports, as well as offering others the chance to introduce themselves if they wish to do so or to give notices of their own. At the end of notices, everyone is invited to the smaller room for a cup of tea or coffee. This week, I have designs on an early lunch and skip that part.

Many things in that description might have seemed strange to someone who had never been to Meeting for Worship. For the purposes of this book, I want to pick out two things which I think are absolutely vital to the process, and also say why I think some of the other stuff that's going on is nice-but-irrelevant. The two vital elements are the gathering or meeting – being with a group – and the unplanned mix of both space (silence, waiting) and communication. Other things, like sitting in a circle, having a plain room, having flowers, sitting for an hour, shaking hands, and so on, are traditional and can be helpful, but I regard them as optional.

Why gather with a group? Obviously, you can sit in silence on your own. Actually, many Quakers do – either just in silence, or using some other spiritual practice, such as Bible reading, mindfulness meditation, contemplative prayer, and so on.

Somehow it isn't the same, though. Worshipping with a group opens up all sorts of possibilities which aren't there when you're alone. For example, someone else might be led to give a message in spoken ministry which is actually for you. As a group, we might be more able to get past our own stuff and find out what God is really asking us to do – this is the core of how Quakers make decisions, described in the next chapter. For some Quakers, the words of Jesus are important and prompt them to gather in worship: 'For where two or three are gathered in my name, I am there among them' (Matthew 18:20, NRSV). I would say that you can't fully understand the power of getting together in unprogrammed worship unless you try it – fortunately it's free and requires no equipment except some willing people.

Why have unprogrammed worship? Why not plan at least some of it? Well, to be honest, there usually is a bit of a plan. It includes things like the start and finish times of the worship (these days normally an hour apart, but anything from five minutes to five hours is known), and some more or less explicit guidelines about giving spoken ministry (usually things like: leave space between contributions, don't speak more than once, and don't give an advert or campaign for a political party). Within that, though, a lot of things could happen. The main reason for being unprogrammed is to leave space for the movement of the Spirit, for the Divine Mystery to lead those present to do whatever is right in that time and place. If that sounds risky – it is. People do sometimes try and exploit it. That's why there are *some* rules about what is allowed. The benefits require the risk, though. Anyone who's been on a date knows that vulnerability comes hand in hand with finding love, and God's Love also requires us to be open to it.

That said, if you go on lots of dates with the same person you start to get a picture of what's most likely to happen. Things which commonly happen in unprogrammed Quaker worship include:

- Someone reading something out, either from a Quaker text or the Bible
- Someone describing something which happened to them (or to someone else) which made them think or understand something better
- Someone mentioning a difficult (or good) situation which needs prayer, sometimes called 'upholding' or 'holding in the Light'
- Someone nodding off
- Something you've been sitting with for a while suddenly seems different: you are clearer about it or find a new angle on it
- Something you haven't thought about in ages pops into your head
- Despite your best efforts you are actually dwelling on something minor – which might turn out to be the thing you see in a new way

Things which happen less often, but I have known, include:

- Someone sings (and other people may or may not join in)
- Someone cries
- Someone has to pop out to use the toilet or answer their phone
- Someone moves – to a different chair, to do their back stretches, to sit on the floor instead, or similar
- Someone speaks more than once (usually this is strongly discouraged, but perhaps they sat down before they were finished)
- Someone speaks for a long time
- Someone speaks for a long time and someone else stops them, perhaps with a phrase like, 'Friend, you have been heard'
- Someone breaks another rule, like naming a political

party, and is stopped

- There's an emergency and the meeting finishes early to deal with it (for example, if someone is taken ill or the fire alarm goes)
- There's a strange noise but everyone ignores it and carries on worshipping (it often turns out that regulars know what it is!)
- There's a noise or something outside and one person goes out to investigate, leaving everyone else to worship (if someone comes to the door, for example)

It's tempting to think of some of these as problems. Certainly some – like the strange noises! – a group might choose to try and get rid of. Others, like ministry delivered in song, might be seen as a great gift by some groups. For myself I try and think of them all as part of the richness and complexity of belonging to a community which belongs to God.

Beyond these reasons for using unprogrammed worship, though, there might be other ways to benefit from this mix of silence and speech. Knowing that we can worship in silence takes the emphasis off words. We don't have to all agree on the same form of words, leaving us free to explore different ways of understanding without having to keep saying something which may not be true for everyone at all times. That relates to the Quaker rejection of written creeds.

On the other hand, we aren't stuck in silence. It's a tool, not a rule. People can speak when they feel led to do so, and that means that Quakers are free to share experiences, offer teaching or reflections, or speak up about injustice or other problems. Seen in this way, ministry – not just things people say in meeting for worship, but actions they might be led to take in their lives, ranging from writing letters to protesting arms sales to knitting socks to volunteering at foodbanks to a thousand others things – comes out of the silence. In Quaker worship, we open ourselves up to be guided and that guidance might lead us in many different directions.

All very well, you might now be thinking, but what about the other stuff? Why meet in meeting houses? Why sit in a circle? Why have flowers in the middle and shake hands at the end? The truth is, these things are there because they are useful or nice, and they can be changed. Gathering, lack of planning, silence, and openness to ministry can't really be changed – if you changed one or all of them, you might still have worship and it might even be Quaker, but it wouldn't be unprogrammed Quaker meeting for worship. No gathering, no meeting. Add planning, not unprogrammed. Remove silence… well, you can meet in a noisy place, but the people who are participating need to find some kind of silence or stillness in order to be open. Ban ministry, and you've taken away one of the main reasons for gathering in the first place. Everything else, on the other hand, is optional.

For example, you need a place to meet. If you own a meeting house, that's handy – but barns, people's homes, hospitals, fields, beaches, chapels, online meeting rooms, gardens, and city centres can all work, too. It's now usual to sit in a circle, but benches are usually in a square or rectangle, and lines, ovals, and all sorts of wobbly as-it-comes shapes are also fine. It's helpful, but not strictly necessary, to be able to see/hear/ sense one another's presence. Putting flowers and books, and maybe a water jug, on a table in the middle is often practical and attractive, but it would still be meeting for worship without. They can help people to settle down – to read for a while or gaze at something beautiful can be useful in getting into the silence – but they can also be distractions. Finally, it is necessary to have a signal that the meeting is finished. A handshake is practical, quiet, friendly, and often inclusive, as everyone present turns to their neighbours in greeting. A verbal or visual signal can work just as well, especially if those present know what to expect, and might be a positive improvement in some cases (don't shake hands if you are risking sharing germs that way!).

Quakers worship in silence because it gives space for them to be open to the Spirit. Unprogrammed worship makes all people equal and puts God in charge.

If you want to find out more about Quaker worship, you could try:

- visiting a Quaker meeting – there's nothing like doing it for real, and this website will help you find Quakers nearby: http://www.quakerinfo.org/quakerism/findingfriends
- listening to a podcast – in 2018, the Young Quaker podcast recorded a meeting for worship: https://youngquakerpodcast.libsyn.com/4-silence-special
- join a Quaker meeting online – there are several options for this, including the one run by Woodbrooke: https://www.woodbrooke.org.uk/about/online-mfw/ and one run by the Ben Lomond Quaker Center: http://www.quakercenter.org/meeting-for-worship/

How many kinds of Quakers are there?

Just two – my kind and the wrong kind!

That's a joke, by the way. I tell it here because it gives you some idea that even though Quakers work hard to create peace, the Quaker movement has had its fair share of splits and disagreements over the three and a half centuries they have been around. In the last chapter, I said that in this book I am mainly going to be discussing unprogrammed Quakers, sometimes also called, confusingly, liberal or conservative Quakers. In this chapter, I want to give you a very brief tour of all the kinds of Quakers, mainly to try and help you get your bearings if you meet some Quakers who aren't much like my descriptions. On the way, I'll introduce some of the labels which are used for them internally, but I'm going to focus on the things about them you might notice. Here are three ways in which Quakers vary: form of worship (programmed or unprogrammed), way of knowing about God (whether the emphasis is on the Bible's teaching or the Inner Light), and approach to the rest of the world (separatist or evangelical).

Unprogrammed or programmed worship

Worship which is unplanned, with lots of silence and people speaking when they are led to speak, is characteristic of unprogrammed Quakers. Programmed worship can include silence and unplanned prayers, but it will also have Bible readings and singing. In general, unprogrammed worship tends to go with a liberal attitude to theology, and programmed worship goes with a stronger emphasis on Christianity and the Bible. The term 'conservative' in reference to Quakers usually refers to worship – conservative and maintaining unprogrammed worship. It can go with more or less liberal attitudes to theology and politics.

Inner Light or Biblical teaching

The core question here is 'how do we know about God?' Early Quakers held that the Holy Spirit, also called Christ Within or the Inward light, speaking directly to people now, would say the same things the Bible says, because they come from the same source – God. Since then, some Quakers have leaned harder on the inward messages and less on the Bible, especially after historical work on biblical texts showed that it was written and edited by human hands. Other Quakers have leaned harder on the Bible and become more suspicious of individual leadings, especially if they might be the work of the person's own desires or something darker. Both positions can be justified as 'Quaker' from earlier writings. In general, focus on the inner light goes with unprogrammed worship, and focus on the Bible goes with programmed worship. However, this is an area where individuals can have beliefs which are different from others in their community, and there can be a lot of variation in a single meeting.

Quietist or Evangelical

'Quietist' is a historian's term, not a Quaker's word for themselves, but I like it because it's very evocative of one stream of Quaker thought. This is a stream which wants to be different and apart from the world, which doesn't want to say much – perhaps not even to other Quakers, and certainly not to non-Quakers. It might also be called 'separatist', wanting to keep non-Quakers at arm's length from Quaker stuff. Evangelical is a good Christian word, describing people who want to actively spread the Good News, whether that's a general Christian message or a specifically Quaker one. Evangelical thought in Quakerism is often associated with programmed worship and Bible-focussed theology, but it also isn't that simple. Some groups of liberal Quakers who use unprogrammed worship have developed a strong tradition of 'outreach', which encourages Quakers to talk

19

to non-Quakers about Quakerism clearly and confidently while not making any specific attempt to persuade them to *become* Quakers. (I belong to that tradition, or I wouldn't be writing this book!)

As well as combinations and overlaps which show that each of these pairs isn't really an opposition, there are also more variations within each group. There are divisions among Quakers over moral questions – for example, although some Quakers are very accepting of homosexuality and have campaigned for same-sex marriage, other Quakers feel that homosexuality is wrong. There are divisions among Quakers over theological issues – for example, among Quakers who are heavily focussed on the leadings of the Inner Light, there can be intense debate about the nature of that Light. Is the Light inherently linked to Christ, or is it equally visible in all religions? Is it an inward Light, shining on us from an external source, or an internal Light, part of our humanity and not coming from a supernatural deity? (For more about this issue, see the chapter 'What's this about Quakers who don't believe in God?') And like any community, Quakers can come into conflict over practical questions, whether that's 'should we refurbish the meeting house kitchen?' or 'is it sensible to invest in solar panels?' or 'how should we handle John who keeps saying inappropriate things?'

At the beginning of this chapter, I told a joke which probably gives the smallest possible number of kinds of Quakers: two. At the other extreme, in 2017 the Friends World Committee for Consultation thought there were about 378,000 Quakers worldwide, and there could be as many kinds of Quakerism as there are Quakers. More usefully, there are probably four broad strands:

- 'Conservative' (unprogrammed worship, balance of Bible and Inner Light, mixed attitudes to the non-Quaker world)
- 'Liberal' (unprogrammed worship, emphasis on Inner

Light, generally open to the non-Quaker world)
- 'Evangelical' (programmed worship, emphasis on the Bible, actively telling non-Quakers about Christianity)
- 'Convergent' (a recent movement trying to bring together the best of different forms of Quakerism, so some of all the above)

To find out more about the many kinds of Quakers in the world, you could:

- explore the Friends World Committee for Consultation website: http://fwcc.world/kinds-of-friends
- watch a video about the difference between programmed and unprogrammed worship: http://quakerspeak.com/difference-between-programmed-unprogrammed-quaker-worship/

How do you know if something you're led to say is really from God?

Most descriptions of unprogrammed Quaker worship include the idea that what people say, when they feel moved to speak into the silence, comes from God in some way. Quakers have lots of different ideas about what that God might be like – a person, not a person, close, far away, involved in the world, stand-offish, loving, angry, funny, playful, mysterious, real, external, part of people, non-existent, a story, revealed in the Bible, active as Spirit, creative, absent. Whatever kind of God you believe in, though, you might reasonably be worried about what evidence Quakers have for this claim that the things which are said in meeting for worship come from God. (For more about different Quaker views of God, see the later chapter in this book, 'What's this about Quakers who don't believe in God?'.)

Here are some kinds of evidence Quakers might present:

- internal feelings about what they are given to say
- group agreement – what is said by one person matches what God has said to others
- scriptural agreement – what is said now matches what God said in the past
- rational arguments – what is said is what we'd expect God to say, logically
- fruits of the Spirit – doing what God tells us to do leads to positive outcomes
- None of these are going to give absolute proof. Taken together, some or all of them might be enough to make it reasonable for Quakers to act as if their idea is right, at least until further evidence comes along. Let's look at them each in more detail.

- **internal feelings about what they are given to say**

'It *feels* like it's from God' is perhaps both the most and least popular of these. It's popular because it's easy for the person who is led to speak to sense, and because it's hard for anyone else to argue with. It's unpopular because it's the one which seems most likely to go wrong: if someone is being deceived by their own desires or ego, or lied to by the devil, this sense of rightness and holiness would be included in that fake. It's also the only test which can be made completely internally, in the silence of meeting for worship. Because it's useful but might be unreliable, Quakers might work to try and improve it. For example, an individual can sometimes learn to tell the difference between what they *want* to say, and what they might not want to say but *have* to say because God is asking them to say it. With prayer and patience, someone might be able to work out the difference between a message which is just for that person, a message they'd like to give but shouldn't share in worship, and something they are led to say during worship.

- **group agreement – what is said by one person matches what God has said to others**

Moving beyond the individual's sense, Quakers often use a group test. This can be applied both to spoken ministry in ordinary meeting for worship – Quakers sometimes talk about 'true ministry' and whether the messages 'spoke to' anyone present – and more obviously to things which are said in meeting for worship for business. Spoken ministry doesn't have to speak to (be helpful or relatable) everyone who is in a meeting, but if it doesn't speak to anyone, it's likely someone was misled. In a meeting for worship for business, the sense of testing by the group is clearer because there usually needs to be a decision or at least enough of an agreement to record in writing.

- scriptural agreement – what is said now matches what God said in the past

A group test doesn't have to be restricted to those who are present. Texts, usually but not always from the Bible, can be used to provide another test. How much this is used by Quakers today depends on their understanding of what the Bible is – it's common in some places and rare in others. Quakers might also use previous Quaker writings as a similar test. Both of these rely on the same argument: if God is saying to Quakers now something which is in keeping with what God said to people in the past, it's more likely to be authentic. This isn't the final test, though, for two reasons. One is that most Quakers think revelation can continue, that is, God can send new and different messages to us today. Evidence for this might be found in changing attitudes both among Quakers and in other faith groups, such as other Christian churches, towards ethical issues – the move by most Christians from an acceptance of slavery to its rejection would be one such example. The other reason texts from the Bible, early Quakers, and other sources can't be a final test is that they are too complex and sometimes contradict themselves or each other. For example, the Quaker practice of treating women equally with men can be supported by some biblical passages and the writings of some early Quakers, but there are also ways in which historically, Quaker women have not been treated equally ('women's meetings' and 'men's meetings' may or may not actually have the same level of influence on the community), and biblical passages in which women are told that they should behave differently to men.

- rational arguments – what is said is what we'd expect God to say, logically

Instead, Quakers might try a rational test. Based on what we know about God from other sources, is this new message in line with what we would expect God to say? If God is loving, for example, we would expect God to give loving messages. This might support apparently new messages which encourage us to extend our love to groups who have previously not be included or treated equally. This test still has a problem with foundations (where do we find out about God in the first place?), which Quakers might choose to answer by pointing to the other tests. Individual religious experiences, together with communal testing of religious messages, both in the present and across time, provide a collective base from which we can move forward. Messages which don't fit – for example, which say we should hate or fear people rather than loving and valuing them – are likely to come from somewhere other than God, whether that's the individual's own fears and struggles, the devil, or somewhere else.

- **fruits of the Spirit – doing what God tells us to do leads to positive outcomes**

A similar test is suggested in the teachings of Jesus.

> Beware of false prophets, who come to you in sheep's clothing but inwardly are ravenous wolves. You will know them by their fruits. Are grapes gathered from thorns, or figs from thistles? (Matthew 7:15–16, New Revised Standard Version)

Here, instead of trying to work out rationally or by individual or group sense whether something has come from God, the messages – words of the prophets – are tested by their results. What is the outcome? If the message leads to positive outcomes, whether that is justice, joy, peace, equality, or similar, it seems to have come from a good source. Sometimes this can be seen immediately. For example, I have heard pieces of spoken ministry in meeting for worship which put a new perspective on something, perhaps events in the news, and enabled me to take a more constructive approach to them straight away. Sometimes it needs trying out. A proposal for a new piece of Quaker work might need to go through a long process of group testing, pilots, and other experiments before it becomes clear that it is true ministry and will produce good fruit.

For any particular idea, perhaps we can never be entirely sure where it came from. Using these tests, though, Quakers are confident enough to speak up, try things out, and share ideas, hoping that even if some fail, many will turn out to be useful in some way.

To find out more about spoken ministry and Quaker work, you could:

- read this webpage from Maury River Friends Meeting who have included some description and some quotes from historical Quakers: https://www.fgcquaker.org/cloud/maury-river-friends-meeting/pages/spirit-led-vocal-ministry
- read *Through Us, Not From Us*, a booklet about spoken ministry published by a British Quaker group, the Kindlers: https://bookshop.quaker.org.uk/through-us-not-from-us-vocal-ministry-and-quaker-worship_9780956224590

Why do Quakers make decisions in worship?

This question could have been replaced by a number of others I've been asked, such as: Why does it take Quakers so long to make decisions? Why are Quakers not democratic? Why do these Quakers say God has told them to do something without giving biblical evidence for that? Quaker decision making – which is seen as a form of discernment, a process of coming to see the right way forward for the group – can be slow, but tries to include all voices equally; can go against what some people, even the majority, personally want, but tries to work out what the community are being led to do on the spiritual level; and can lead to surprising outcomes, based on a deeply-rooted faith but open to new revelation.

What is actually involved? A Quaker decision-making meeting in session starts out with a lot in common with an ordinary meeting for worship. Indeed, it's sometimes called a meeting for worship for business, or a meeting for worship for church affairs. At my local Quaker meeting, when we want to make decisions, we rearrange the furniture slightly – so that the two people who have been asked to clerk the meeting (a bit like chairing) can have a table. Otherwise, we use the same set up as for worship, seated in a circle. It's also a bit like a committee meeting in any other walk of life: we have an agenda, which has been suggested in advance by our clerks; we have a target amount of time to get through the business, although we might leave some until later if necessary; and we come as people, with our ideas and thoughts and feelings and opinions.

The meeting for worship for business starts with worship, open to spoken contributions but usually mainly silent. This is time during which those attending can settle themselves, try to become aware of and set aside anything which might affect their participation in the business, and seek to be open to the guiding Light of the God who leads us. After this opening worship the clerk introduces the first item of business. For this example, let's imagine the meeting has been asked to send a representative to another meeting for worship for business. This sort of item is often straightforward. The clerk reminds the meeting about when and where the other event is, and why someone should attend. In some cases, a small group of people will have already found and suggested someone who would be willing to go, in which case the meeting considers whether that person is the right person. (If that sounds bizarre, skip ahead to 'Why don't Quakers volunteer for roles within the Quaker community?' to read about nominations committees.) In other cases, anyone present at the current meeting might be suitable to attend, or several could go, in which case the clerk might just ask people to indicate if they are planning to go anyway, to offer to go, or to suggest someone else who might be willing to go. In every case, the aim is to balance practicality – Brenda is going in her car so can give lifts to some others – with openness to inspiration – Bob has never attended this kind of meeting before but something in this agenda attracts him.

Once someone is appointed, the clerk notes that down. Depending on the tradition, she might read out what she has written immediately, so that the whole meeting is clear and can correct the record, known as the minute, if necessary. Now the decision has been made, and perhaps after a short period of worship, the next item is introduced.

For a more complex decision, more time might be needed. Some decisions are brought to the meeting after lots of preparation work by a committee. For example, the yearly budget is usually brought to the whole meeting for approval, but a treasurer, finance committee, and professional accountant may all have been involved in creating it. Other questions come to the meeting for decision but turn out to need more research or discussion, and in those cases the meeting might ask a group to look into it and come back, or hold a 'threshing meeting', a space when views can be aired on a topic but there is no attempt to reach a conclusion. Whichever process is used, the emphasis is on finding the right way forward through the core method of listening to God's voice as articulated by people within the community.

People who hear about this way of making decisions are sometimes horrified that it isn't democratic. I've also heard it described as super-democratic. Both people think that being democratic is a good thing – it's a word which has become attached to 'good ways of doing government'. In the context of governing a nation, democracy using voting is a good idea because it's fair, includes everyone equally, and so on. (Obviously any actual system usually falls short of these ideals: only some people can vote, representative systems don't give everyone a say on everything, first past the post voting means not every vote is equally significant, etc. The ideals are what matter here!) In the context of a Quaker community, similar ideals about fairness, equality, and including everyone are in play, but there are also hesitations about voting as a method and another ideal, about finding a way forward which is *right* even if it isn't what people *want*. Let me unpack those a bit.

Democracy, rule by the people, doesn't automatically mean voting. A consensus system, in which everyone has a say and a compromise is sought, could also be democratic. And voting can create problems. In particular, if you vote yes/no on an issue and the majority say yes, everyone who said no is left out. Sometimes you can handle that – a youth group I worked with sometimes voted on which game to play, but if the vote went for Wink Murder one week those who wanted Cat and Mouse were usually happy that they would win next week. At other times this division between 'winners' and 'losers' can become entrenched and make it difficult to consider other solutions, keep lines of communication open, and find a way forward which works for everyone. As I write this the UK government are trying to sort out Brexit, a case in which a national referendum already left many people feeling the nation was split, and where Parliament's own voting system isn't clarifying the matter as people repeatedly vote to reject all possible options. The Quaker way of making decisions tries to hear from all perspectives but to avoid the divisive effects of voting.

The Quaker way of making decisions also doesn't really aim to be democratic. It wants to involve all the people, not so much for themselves, but because each of them has a unique access to the Divine. It is theocratic, ruled by God. The word 'theocratic' has also been used to mean rule by a priesthood, and we could say that this is also true of Quakers – accepting that for Quakers, the priesthood of all believers means that a theocracy ruled by priests and a democracy ruled by the people would come out to rule by the same set of individuals. In a Quaker meeting for worship for business, everyone present tries to set aside their personal desires and focus on finding the right way forward. I think we all have experience of distinguishing our wants from our needs: I want to watch TV all day, but I need to clean the house. Quakers add a third level, for both individual and community: what we want, what we need, and what God wants. Quakers meeting together sometimes reach extraordinary, even apparently irrational, conclusions in which the personal desires of those present are set aside in the service of some much larger goal. I've heard of meetings who buy property to welcome refugees, take dramatic steps to becoming more environmentally friendly, or are called to protest against or even break unjust laws.

To find out more about how Quakers make decisions, you could:

- watch this video from QuakerSpeak in which Eden Grace

discusses the process: http://quakerspeak.com/quaker-decision-making-consensus/

- read this article from *Friends Journal* in which Arthur Meyer Boyd talks about what happens when Quakers disagree: https://www.friendsjournal.org/2010090/
- go into more depth with a book like *God and Decision-Making* by Jane Mace (Quaker Books, 2012): https://bookshop.quaker.org.uk/god-and-decision-making_9781907123320

What's this about Quakers who don't believe in God?

Religious people believe in God. In the English-speaking world, this is probably one of the most widely assumed facts about religion. Even after learning about religious traditions which do not focus on or believe in God, or which worship many deities, it's usual to go on taking 'belief in God' as central to the idea of a religion. That's partly because of the history of the idea of religion in Europe and America, where 'religion' starts out as a synonym for Christianity, often Protestant Christianity, and is widened from there to include other faiths. It's also because teaching and media discussion about religion focusses on God, whether that's in a story about famous atheists rejecting God or trying to explain Islam through a stereotyped picture in which the word 'Allah', Arabic for God, features prominently. Under this influence, although most people know about the existence of religions in which god or gods are non-existent or downplayed – the most common example is Buddhism, which is complex but certainly very different to Christianity, Judaism, or Islam – that isn't what comes to mind first when they think of religion. This isn't surprising, because our minds focus on the most typical examples first (performers have built whole 'mind reading' stage routines on predicting reliably how many people will say 'robin' when asked to name a bird and 'carrot' when asked to name a vegetable). It does mean that even people who have studied religion to a fairly advanced level are sometimes taken by surprise when I say that Quakers don't all believe in God.

Let me clarify what is being claimed here. I'm saying that not all Quakers believe in God – NOT that all Quakers have rejected God (that certainly isn't the case). I'm saying that Quakers who don't believe in God are proper, real Quakers – not just that some people associated with Quaker communities are also atheists. I'm saying that being able to honestly make a statement like 'I believe in God' isn't vital to becoming a Quaker – but not that belief, worship, faith, religious experience, and other related concepts are irrelevant to understanding Quakerism.

Quakers who don't believe in God, most of whom call themselves nontheist Quakers, vary hugely in what they *do* believe: both in what they think exists in the world, and in what they think happens during Meeting for Worship. Some believe in something more-than-physical but reject the word 'God' for it as misleading or dishonest. Some favour fully materialist explanations, others are happy with concepts like the soul or collective energy of a group, and others are strongly into psychological approaches to religion. Nontheists do not automatically reject prayer, mysticism, or Jesus. For some, a 'Divine' might exist but is so mysterious it would be wrong to try and say anything about it. For others, God is a social rather than a physical reality: 'Real Like I Love You', in the words of a well-known nontheist book title.

When people start to understand this about Quakers, questions they often ask include:

- Are the Quakers who do believe in God okay with this?
- What effect does it have on the community?
- Isn't it just about how people describe their experiences?
- But don't you need God in order to have Quakerism?

I'll take those one at a time.

Quakers who do believe in God have mixed reactions to nontheism, depending on their tradition, circumstances, and personal factors. In unprogrammed liberal Quaker traditions, asking questions, doubting, and exploring is sufficiently normalised, often encouraged, that at least having a nontheist phase is usually not seen as a problem. When nontheism begins to be a more permanent feature of the community, some Quakers do find this difficult. For some it feels threatening, especially if they see it as an attempt to move Quakerism away from being a spiritual path towards being something secular. There are significant worries about how someone who does not believe in a God who provides leadings can participate in a Meeting for Worship for Business where the community is trying to work out what God wants them to do. At the same time, nontheist Quakers observably do succeed in participating in Quaker worship, including Quaker decision making. Sometimes it seems that the importance of joining in with Quaker practices is emphasised by an increasing awareness of nontheism. As with so many things, comfort often comes with familiarity, and in many Quakers meetings I know, Quakers who have a wide range of beliefs (or who try to have no beliefs) about God get along just fine.

Oddly, the effect of visible nontheist Quakers might be to make the Quaker community talk more about their many understandings of what God is. The process of shifting from quietly assuming that everyone has similar ideas, to confidently sharing one's own and accepting that others disagree isn't always an easy one. It does mean that Quakers are more frequently encouraged to try and express their current thoughts on theological topics like the nature of God, whether God has a personality and what it might be like, and what happens in meeting for worship. Sometimes disagreements go beyond discussions. People do leave the Quaker community over this when they feel their position is no longer acceptable or insufficiently supported – some because there is not enough room for nontheism, some because they feel God is being pushed out, some because there isn't enough emphasis on Christianity, or for other reasons. However, a lot of liberal Quaker communities are finding ways to include everyone and find positives in this process of exploration.

Some discussion of nontheism has focussed on the language

Quakers use to describe religious and spiritual things. It's reasonable to ask whether, if we ditched the word 'God', it would come out that everyone was describing the same experiences after all. For Quakers, for whom religious experience is very important, this is an especially obvious question. Some take the answer 'yes' for granted, but I think it's not that easy for two reasons. Firstly, the language we use affects our experiences – for a simple example, I approach my first bite of a new food differently if my friend has just described it as 'delicious' or 'an acquired taste' or 'yucky'. Taking away the word God, with all the connotations and associated pictures, might affect the experience itself. Secondly, even when groups of Quakers try and explain their experience without certain words, it still seems that some are describing a positive experience, of connection with the world or the Divine, while others are describing an absence of experience, a sense of the lack of connection. This distinction doesn't map neatly onto people who believe in God and nontheists, actually, plenty of devout believers also have the experience of God's absence, but it does suggest that more is at work than a linguistic issue.

Finally, no, I don't think you need God in order to have Quakerism. Note that this is just my opinion, and there are definitely Quakers who would disagree. All I can do here is very briefly summarise some arguments in each direction. The core question might be put differently, as: 'What is Quakerism?' For some people, the central part of Quakerism is direct experience of God – or maybe something more specific, such as Christ Within. However, an alternative is to say that mystical experience doesn't require belief in God. If that's so, experience of the Inner Light, understood without reference to an external deity, or a personal deity, or whatever other aspect of 'God' someone rejects. For others, the central part of Quakerism is the teaching, whether that's the teaching of George Fox and other Quakers, biblical teachings, or both. However, the core teaching of Quakerism might not be a traditional belief statement, but more about practice, especially of unprogrammed worship. If that's so, participating in Quaker worship without believing in God is still being Quaker.

If you want to know more, you might be overwhelmed with choices. Because this is a contentious issue, lots of people have wanted to say their piece!

- I already wrote about this in more detail in my Quaker Quicks book, *Telling the Truth about God* (John Hunt/ Christian Alternative Press, 2019): https://www. johnhuntpublishing.com/christian-alternative-books/our-books/quaker-quicks-telling-truth-about-god
- Quakers in Britain held a think-tank in 2016 which produced a book of reflections, called *God, Words and Us* (Quaker Books): https://bookshop.quaker.org.uk/God-words-and-us_9781999726928
- Nontheist Quakers have told their own stories: try *Godless for God's Sake*, an anthology of different perspectives, as a starting place (Dales Historical Monographs, 2006): https://bookshop.quaker.org.uk/Godless-for-Gods-Sake_9780951157862
- Sam Barnett-Cormack often writes about these issues on his blog, Quaker Openings: https://quakeropenings.blogspot.com/
- A whole range of views are given in this short video, 'What do Quakers believe about God': https://www.youtube.com/watch?v=4nsEoG7ovZQ

Why don't Quakers do things other churches do, like baptism and the eucharist?

We think those things happen internally, between the person and God, and don't need to be acted out in rituals.

'Don't need to be' doesn't automatically mean 'shouldn't', and there are Quakers, myself included, who will participate in communion or other physical manifestations of inner realities when the Spirit leads. There are also Quakers who disagree about an inner version being enough, or who read the Bible as commanding physical ritual actions, who do baptise with water and celebrate communion. That said, the Quaker rejection of baptism and the eucharist as physical actions puts some interesting light on Quaker ways of thinking generally and is worth exploring in more detail.

In many churches, baptism is a ritual of entering the faith. Whether children are baptised or adults, baptism makes someone into a Christian and, in some theologies, gives them the opportunity to have a right relationship with God. In the absence of baptism, it's reasonable to ask: how do Quakers become Quakers? How do Quakers understand that process of getting things sorted out with God?

Here are three technical terms for us to conjure with in thinking this through: convincement, membership, and salvation.

'Convincement' is a word Quakers use to describe the experience which prompts someone to accept the Quaker world view or embrace a Quaker understanding. It's often used in a similar way to 'conversion', as in converting to a new religion. In the seventeenth century when Quakers were first around, 'convinced' had a meaning something more like 'convicted' today, so it carries hints of being convicted of sin as well as convinced by the truth. A Quaker might talk about their own convincement experience – which might be a single moment or years of growing understanding. A single flash convincement can sound a lot like a 'born again' moment in other Christian traditions. A long period of subtle nudges towards Quakerism might only be visible in hindsight. For those born into Quakerism, it might be more about testing that they find it convincing rather than being able to point to a moment of convincement. However it comes, convincement is a spiritual process, in which heart, mind, and actions are turned to the Divine.

'Membership' is a word used by many Quaker communities to talk about the process by which someone joins the Quaker community. It's still a spiritual process, often following convincement, but also involves testing and acceptance by the Quaker organisation. (For more about Quaker structures, see the chapter on 'Do Quakers have structures like parishes?'.) There might be a more or less active distinction between attenders, people who attend meeting for worship, and members, people who are expected to take a share of the responsibility for organising the community. A lot of variety – about who comes into membership and how, and about how much attenders actually do or are allowed to do – exists even within organised groups of Quakers, let alone in the worldwide Quaker community, so here I recommend you ask locally. All I need to establish for this chapter is that Quakers do have formal structures for trying to recognise who is and who is not a Quaker.

'Salvation' is not a word liberal Quakers use very much. In some Quaker traditions, as in some other Christian traditions, it's a common word, but the very idea can be difficult for liberal Quakers. I used to enjoy making British Quakers uncomfortable by asking them about it directly until one day I pushed too far and made a workshop participant cry. I still ask but I'm more gentle about it now! I think the difficulty comes from an association of the idea of salvation with a picture of the world in which salvation is only open to some people. In my experience of asking directly, Quakers will push back against any idea that salvation is not universal. Often they will prefer to use another word, like 'transformation', which makes it clear that it is an inner process and that anyone can access it.

So where does that leave baptism? In this Quaker understanding, no baptism or any other particular ritual is needed for salvation, because the transformation of a person into someone who is right with God is an inner process. There is a visible process for joining the community, but it's a membership application: it might involve letter writing, conversation, praying together, and meeting for worship for business, but it recognises what the Spirit has already done in bringing someone to Quakerism rather than aiming to make something happen. That process of transformation from non-Quaker to Quaker might take any one of many forms, all known as convincement experiences.

Now someone has become a Quaker, what about the eucharist? 'Take, eat, this is my body'?

The Quaker worry about acting this out is that you might get distracted by the food and the words and all the other interesting stuff, and forget to actually commune with God. For Quakers, pre-planning suggests a lack of response to your real spiritual state in the moment. The eucharist got rejected along with all the rest of a church service: the pre-arranged hymns, choosing a Bible reading in advance, a sermon written the day before, the liturgy set down by higher authority. All this might be empty words, actions made without real thought or feeling, going through the motions, an outward form which does not reflect an inward reality. I think we can all think of times when we have acted on autopilot: said 'Good morning' without considering whether it's really good (or even whether it's actually the morning), turned left towards the office on Saturday morning when you meant to turn right into town, or gone through the motions of a conversation while longing to get out of it and go for dinner. The Quaker accusation about pre-planned church services is that they enable people to act on autopilot in this kind of way, dishonestly seeming to be faithful Christians when they are not actually having the spiritual experiences which should go with the actions.

If you value the rituals of baptism and eucharist, if you write or listen to good sermons or church music, I know that you might reasonably be objecting strenuously at this point. (If you're not, you can skip this paragraph.) Overall, Quakers have cooled down a lot since the early days when these arguments were put most strongly, and although the problems are still there, it's common even in Quaker communities which wouldn't want to use them directly to acknowledge that there are also many positive aspects to liturgy, music, and other prepared contributions to worship. For example, sermon givers will rightly say that preparation helps and they speak spontaneously as well as from notes when the Holy Spirit moves. There are Quakers who agree with you, and even those on the most rejection-of-planning end of the spectrum will usually agree that studying spiritual texts, taking time to prepare heart and mind before worship, and so on, all help with the depth and quality of unprogrammed worship. Similarly, for music-lovers reading this: I know creating music in a group needs planning and practice and is, for some people, a path to spiritual experience. There are Quakers who agree with you, some who include hymns regularly in their worship, and a Quaker musical tradition does exist even where it's rarely part of worship. (Some Quaker groups publish songbooks.) Furthermore, Quakers do have a liturgy, a pattern of worship which is predictable – and can fall into the very patterns of 'empty ritual' which Quakers criticise.

In conclusion, Quakers don't see the need for making baptism and eucharist, or many other rituals, physical. These are inward events between the person and God. Doing things on a schedule might encourage dishonesty about the real situation – the inner, spiritual bit. That said, Quakers don't reject people who have been baptised, and some will participate in communion with physical elements if they are moved by the Spirit to do so.

If you'd like to find out more about Quaker views of what other churches do, you could look at these sources:

- Michael Birkel explores why Quakers don't take communion in this video from QuakerSpeak: http://quakerspeak.com/michael-birkel-form-without-substance/
- Terry Oakley describes unprogrammed Quaker worship in terms of communion in this article in *The Friend*: https://thefriend.org/article/thought-for-the-week-communion-in-meeting
- in 1987, British Quakers produced a response to the World Council of Churches which dealt with baptism, eucharist, and ministry in detail – the document is called *To Lima with Love* and can be found online here: http://hst.name/RSoF/tlwl.pdf

Okay, but what about Christmas and Easter?

This is tricky ground. Historically, Quakers refused to treat Christmas and Easter differently from any other days of the year. The idea is that we remember the birth, teaching, suffering, and death of Jesus every day, so there's no need to mark it out. You might think that it sounds difficult to remember them all equally every day, and that liturgical calendars exist for a reason. You are right. It is also true that Quakers who live in majority Christian societies come under a lot of pressure to conform, especially since it's now common for people to join Quakers as adults and have non-Quaker family.

The facts as I have observed them are that many Quakers celebrate Christmas in a relatively quiet but conventional way. Some unprogrammed meetings hold a meeting for worship on Christmas Day. Some will have a Christmas celebration during December, perhaps including a children's play (not necessarily a traditional Nativity, but 'alterative takes', like a Holy Family who are modern refugees, turn up fairly often) and sometimes including some well-known carols, cake, and other generally-liked things about the way Christmas is celebrated in the surrounding society. Similarly, at home many Quakers participate in traditions like gift giving, tree decorating, sharing meals with family, and donating to charity.

However, not all unprogrammed Quakers are Christian or come from a Christian background. Jewish Quakers, for example, might well maintain their own attitude to Christmas, which could be anything from secular participation to not wanting anything to do with it – and it doesn't always sit well with non-Christian Quakers when other Quakers participate in religious ways of celebrating Christmas. It can seem hypocritical, or a betrayal of earlier Quaker principles. But that history is also a complicating factor. When the Quaker movement began, treating Christmas like any other day was much more widely acceptable, and practically the only thing which is widely remembered about the Puritan movement, also from that time, is that they 'banned Christmas'. Because of that, to refuse to participate in any Christmas customs is seen today in wider society as a deeply anti-social, anti-fun, 'Puritanical' thing to do.

Modern liberal Quakers are counter-cultural in some ways – opposition to all wars, for example – but they have dropped their oppositions to art, music, fiction, and generally see themselves as social, fun, good company. To keep refusing anything to do with Christmas would go very strongly against this wider move. This also helps to explain the strange things which have developed around Easter.

There are some Quakers who find the religious parts of Easter – the torture, death, and resurrection of Jesus Christ – deeply meaningful. There is Meeting for Worship on Easter Sunday (because it's by definition a Sunday, and almost every meeting worships on Sunday even if they also meet at other times), and spoken ministry may or may not include these themes, as those present feel led. There are also a lot of Quakers who do the fun bits of Easter, without worrying about the darker side. For example, many Quaker children will have an Easter Egg hunt – emphasis on the chocolate. (Of course, Quakers do have a historic connection to chocolate, since Cadbury's, Fry's, Rowntree's, and other firms were founded by Quakers, but I'm not sure this justifies a religious involvement now those companies have been sold off!)

This is also a place where it's difficult to be clear because there is a big grey area between what Quakers do as Quakers, and what individual Quakers do as themselves. Quaker meetings don't organise anything special for Lent – where other churches might have study groups or similar – but at least some individual Quakers do either give something up for Lent, or recognise it in some other way, like by giving donations to charity. Most Quaker meetings don't do anything for Good Friday (although I know at least one which does), but individual Quakers might follow some traditions especially if they belong to a family which does. Quaker meetings don't typically do anything for Maundy Thursday, but a lot of Quakers would make pancakes especially if they have children at home, and if a meeting had an event on that Thursday anyway, I wouldn't be at all surprised if they recognised the occasion by serving traditional food. That being so, I can't tell you that Quakers do anything for Easter – but I also can't tell you that they definitely don't.

Similarly, Quakers who are not Christian, especially if they have a previous or parallel connection with another faith community, might as individuals participate in other religious holidays. For example, Jewish Quakers will choose how to participate in Yom Kippur, Pesach, etc. – taking into account many of the same factors Christian Quakers are considering when choosing how and whether to participate in Easter and Christmas traditions, and probably reaching a similar range of conclusions to other Jews who are balancing religion, culture, spirituality, secularism, and so on. The Westernised forms of Buddhism which seem to attract Quakers aren't as strong on special days as some forms of Eastern Buddhism are, but Buddhist Quakers can still have a clash between taking Quaker involvement in Christian festivals as part of Quakerism's Christian heritage and wanting to reject it because the Christian material isn't as relevant to their faith. Where problems arise, the gaps are often smoothed over with a bit of what we could call 'cake universalism' – people are relaxed and will join in with whatever is going on, especially if it's fun and there's food involved.

For more about the complex relationship between Quakers and Christmas, you could look at:

- a blog post I wrote in 2016, *Five Reasons Quakers Can Celebrate Christmas:* https://brigidfoxandbuddha.word press.com/2016/12/12/five-reasons-quakers-can-celebrate-christmas/
- a very different blog post from Mark Russ, also written earlier in 2016, called *Nourished with Emptiness*: https://jollyquaker.com/2016/02/02/nourished-with-emptiness/
- an article in *Friends Journal* from Jack H. Schick which reports one meeting's annual struggle about whether to have a Christmas tree: https://www.friendsjournal.org/some-friends-will-have-a-christmas-tree/

What about special occasions, like weddings and funerals?

Like other communities, Quakers recognise these life events. The ways in which the Quaker versions are different from others might help to shed light on what Quakers consider to be important. I'll talk about weddings and funerals separately, although many of the same themes will come up in both cases.

A Quaker wedding is based on a meeting for worship. Most of the time is spent in unprogrammed worship – family and friends are free to speak, and often do, leaving gaps between contributions just as in an ordinary Quaker meeting for worship. (See the chapter on 'Why do Quakers worship in silence?' for details.) There are some planned bits, though. Most importantly, the couple will have agreed on their vows in advance. They give their vows as spoken ministry. Someone is appointed to deal with the paperwork – a registering officer or other job title depending on local laws – but nobody else marries the couple: they marry each other, or God marries them and the Quaker wedding recognises this fact in public.

At the end of meeting for worship, it's usual for the couple to sign a marriage certificate, followed by everyone else who is present. This tradition comes from a time when Quaker weddings were not recognised by the law, so Quakers got as many witnesses as possible and kept good records in order to be able to show that they were indeed married under their own religious rules if it ever came to court. There were several cases in Britain where it did, especially where inheritance was involved, and judges ruled that Quaker marriages should be recognised even before the law was changed to allow Quakers to register their marriages with the state.

More recently, some Yearly Meetings have decided to practise equal marriage, treating same-gender couples in the same way as different-gender couples. This is not universal among Quakers, but there are a number of places where Quakers have been active in campaigns for the legalisation of (what laws usually call) same-sex marriage and for better treatment of gay, lesbian, and bisexual people. The history of Quaker marriages recognised as true marriages by Quakers, even when the law did not recognise them, has sometimes been used to justify meetings which celebrate marriages between same-gender couples whose relationships are not recognised in law. The other key argument in this discussion rests on the idea that marriages are not made by human hands, but are God's work: Quakers find that there are couples in our meetings who are married, spiritually speaking, and we recognise this even when the law does not.

Outside the meeting for worship and any legal elements, Quaker weddings can be tailored to suit the couple and the Quaker community involved. In some places, it is usual for there to be a 'meeting for clearness' some time before the wedding – this is a space where the couple and a handful of other Quakers can explore what it means to get married, why the couple want a Quaker wedding, and whether this is the right time. After the wedding, there might be a big dinner with catering laid on, or a simple shared lunch where everyone brings something. There's unlikely to be alcohol – usually not allowed on Quaker-owned premises – but exceptions are sometimes made for a small amount or the couple might move on to another venue. Many Quaker couples choose simpler and cheaper options, but they are free to use traditions which matter to them: one bride might want the white dress, while another couple really want rings, and another groom needs to give space for his dear friend to give a 'best man' speech (even though a Quaker wedding doesn't need a best man as such). Similarly, people attending a Quaker wedding can dress up, or not, as they like.

Quaker funerals and memorial meetings work in a similar way: based on the principles of meeting for worship (waiting and listening to God and each other), people do what needs to be done while also making space for the Spirit to move. Again, it can be customised, and especially if there are non-Quaker family or friends involved there may be elements from other traditions, planned or unplanned. To meet different people's needs, there can be more than one event. For example, there might be a ceremony at the funeral for close family, especially if many or all of them are not Quakers, drawing on whichever traditions are meaningful to them, and later a memorial meeting at which Quaker friends and family can remember the deceased person in their own way. When I say 'later', the memorial meeting can be anything from hours to months later, depending on the needs of the people and communities involved.

In a purely Quaker funeral or memorial meeting, most of the time is spent in unprogrammed worship. Preparing something to say may be more acceptable than usual, especially for those who are deepest in grief, but there is still the expectation of silence and being led to speak. People might be more honest than in some other funeral traditions, because truth is important to Quakers. There may or may not be any talk about heaven or other forms of life after death – generally speaking, unprogrammed Quakers are theologically liberal and have little to say about this. For some it is important, for others irrelevant or even silly, and for most it is private. The focus is more likely to be on the life of the deceased person, especially on articulating the ways in which they were able to be true to their leadings or share their Inner Light with others. Sometimes meetings decide to formalise this in a written document called 'A Testimony to the Grace of God in the Life of...'.

Like any caring community, Quakers aim to support those who are bereaved (or in other forms of difficulty) and offer spiritual and emotional as well as practical care. Unfortunately, I have heard too many stories about times when this has been missed or someone has felt unsupported to be able to tell you that this will happen reliably. It's something we keep working on within the community. If you have – or the person who died had – any level of involvement in a Quaker community, I encourage you to let people know what is happening and ask for support if that seems appropriate.

Besides weddings and funerals, Quaker communities might choose to hold meetings for worship around other life events. Although there is no ritual of outward baptism, some Quaker parents choose to ask for a 'welcome meeting' for their young children (and new arrivals are usually visited by someone from the meeting community even if there is no specific gathering). Quakers don't necessarily have engagements before getting married, and expensive rings are definitely not needed, but I have heard of a Quaker engagement party. When I held a coming out party, I included some elements inspired by Quaker traditions, like a poster which was signed by everyone present as witnesses. Quakers also have ordinary parties with no particular Quaker elements – a birthday party for a Quaker might have a moment of silence when the meal is served, but it might not, and it might be completely identical to a party for a non-Quaker.

To find out more about Quaker weddings, you might like to look at these sources:

- a blog post by Michael Booth about what to expect at a Quaker wedding: http://www.quaker.org.uk/blog/what-to-expect-from-a-quaker-wedding
- a post on The Knot about Quaker wedding ceremonies: https://www.theknot.com/content/quaker-wedding-ceremony-rituals
- a video from Jessica Kellgren-Fozard about her own Quaker wedding: https://www.youtube.com/watch?v=yAtQf-60Lhs
- To find out more about Quaker funerals, you might like to look at these sources:

- a blog post by Paul Parker about what happens at a Quaker funeral: https://www.quaker.org.uk/blog/quaker-funerals
- a post on the Good Funeral Guide about Quaker and atheist funerals: https://www.goodfuneralguide.co.uk/2012/06/what-quakers-atheists-common/
- a video from QuakerSpeaks about why Quaker cemeteries are different: http://quakerspeak.com/how-are-quaker-cemeteries-different/

Do Quakers wear special clothes or anything?

At some times they have, but now they mostly don't.

I kept 'or anything' in this question because as well as distinctive forms of dress, Quakers in some times and places have had distinctive ways of acting and speaking. Today, you probably couldn't pick a Quaker out of a crowd of people from a similar social and economic background, but at some times in history the differences have been stark. The distinctive Quaker way of dressing started out as an attempt to be plain and simple. Quakers wore grey because it was hard-wearing (better than white) and didn't need too much dye (unlike black). The rest was just the standard style of the time – although it has been suggested that Quakers began to show their wealth through their dress even within the restrictions of simplicity. For example, you can buy a very plain coat which is made of very good quality cloth, and everyone can see that you're rich at the same time as you are obviously trying to dress 'simply'.

A few individual Quakers now adopt obvious plain dress, like head coverings or only wearing one style of garment. Many more wear the same styles of clothes as everyone else around them, although they might have a personal rule about simplicity. For example, I know some Quakers who actively choose unbranded clothes so that the presence of big-name brands doesn't become a way to show off. Others might be paying attention to other questions about clothes – are the people who make them paid fairly? Is the fabric as environmentally friendly as possible?

The tradition of 'plain speech' usually describes the old Quaker habit of addressing everyone using 'thee' and 'thou'. When Quakerism began, English speakers used the singular 'thee' and 'thou' for intimates and social inferiors, and the plural 'you' as a polite form for social superiors. Quakers opposed this because – like titles, taking off your hat to certain people, and other superficial polite forms – it encouraged inequality in society. Instead, they wanted to treat everyone equally, and that meant using 'thee' and 'thou' for everyone. Since the seventeenth century, speakers of English as a group have basically agreed with Quakers, except instead of demoting everyone to 'thee' they have promoted everyone to 'you'. Seeing this, almost all Quaker English speakers now go with the flow and use 'you' for everyone – like everyone else who speaks modern English.

Older forms, including 'thee' and 'thou' do linger in some well-known Quaker phrases – in quotations from George Fox, for example, like 'You will say, Christ saith this, and the apostles say this: but what canst thou say?' On the whole, though, even these are often updated when quoted in speech and informal situations, since the archaic grammar is more likely to prevent people understanding the point than to help them get it. Some other kinds of plain speech, like not using titles, are still widespread among Quakers. Again, refusing to use titles is about treating everyone as equals, when a system of titles specifically works to create differences between people. Instead, the polite Quaker form is to use someone's plain name, so that I would be addressed as 'Rhiannon Grant' – rather than just 'Rhiannon', which is over familiar from a stranger; or just 'Grant' which might be brusque or confusing; or Mr Grant or Mrs Grant or Miss Grant or Ms Grant or Mx Grant, which require the speaker to either know my gender and marital status or guess about them, and by giving those forms of information suggests that they matter; or Dr Grant or Professor Grant or something else, which again require the speaker to have prior information about me and suggests that information is important. A while ago I was in a conversation with some people who were arguing that using titles is just a matter of politeness and it wouldn't affect how anyone was treated. During that conversation, I revealed that my 'correct' title in non-Quaker terms is Dr Grant, because I have a

PhD. When I realised that they were taking much more notice of my opinions after discovering my educational background, I decided that – contrary to their arguments – at least some titles were affecting how they treated people!

I put 'correct' in scare quotes there because I'm a Quaker and I prefer not to use a title. I don't usually make a fuss, so people assign me whatever title they like, but as a result of free-text boxes in online forms I do get some post addressed to 'None Rhiannon Grant'.

There's also a kind of plain speaking which isn't about the specific words, but about being honest and taking answers at face value, speaking simply and straightforwardly, and that's still common, too. If a Quaker asks you whether you want some cake, say 'yes' if you want some and 'no' if you don't – they may not be willing to play a game of polite demurrals and encouragements. Sometimes this can seem like being overly blunt or even rude (and sometimes it's an excuse for actually being rude). In other situations, like pointing out the obvious in political debates, it can be a powerful truth-telling technique.

What about other forms of 'or anything'? Quakers don't have secret handshakes. At one time there was apparently a distinctive Quaker way of walking, very purposeful and not graceful, but I suspect social norms about movement have changed and made that irrelevant. The ways that do exist to pick out a Quaker are often very subtle. For example, if someone mentions going to meeting – just meeting, with no article, rather than *the* meeting or *a* meeting – there's a fair chance that Quaker meeting for worship is what's meant. On the other hand, if you think you've found a Quaker, why not just ask? Quakers value honesty and will tell you if you're right.

For more about plain dress and plain speaking, you could:

- explore the website of a plain-dressing Quaker, http://quakerjane.com/

- watch a video about the history of plain speech: http://quakerspeak.com/history-quaker-plain-speech/
- read an article by Anne de Grunchy about 'complex simplicity': https://thefriend.org/article/simplicity-complex-simplicity

Do Quakers have structures like parishes?

Yes. Exactly how things are arranged varies around the world – as I think it does in most churches – especially to take account of local needs, geography, and the density of Quakers. For example, I live in the southern part of the UK city of Birmingham, an area with a rich Quaker history (that's rich as in interesting but also rich as in dripping with cash: the Cadbury family did well out of their chocolate business). Within two miles of where I sit now, there are at least five places where Quaker meeting for worship is held regularly. That amount of Quaker activity supports a significant amount of Quaker structure: the same area includes three Local Meetings, all of which happen to meet in their own meeting houses, and which belong to an Area Meeting covering the whole city and some surrounding areas. The Area Meeting belongs to Britain Yearly Meeting.

In other places there might only be a Worshipping Group, or a Monthly Meeting (big enough to need to hold a meeting for worship for business and maybe, like an Area Meeting, to have smaller meetings which belong to it). Most but not all Quaker meetings belong to a Yearly Meeting, which you might think of as the middle of a nesting set of meetings, or the top of a pyramid of meetings, or a kind of processing centre where smaller meetings send in suggestions and ideas for sorting, further discernment, or approval, and the Yearly Meeting considers them and sends them out again.

Let's stick with that first image, of the meetings as a set of nesting dolls, for a little while. On the outside we have some tissue paper the dolls have been wrapped in – that's Friends World Committee for Consultation, not really a meeting as such but something which unites as many Yearly Meetings as it can (or wraps up as many sets of nesting dolls as possible). Friends World Committee for Consultation creates world gatherings from time to time, tries to keep in touch with lone Quakers and small meetings which are outside the structures (little dolls which don't have bigger dolls to keep them safe), and generally facilitates communication – hence the name – but it doesn't have any authority over anyone, which is why it's not a doll in itself.

Inside the tissue paper, the first and biggest doll is the Yearly Meeting. Most of these have annual sessions, hence the name. Of course, reality isn't always so tidy, and if you picked a Yearly Meeting at random you might find that it met every eighteen months, or sometimes got together twice in a year, or had 'continuing sessions' between meetings. Depending on the location, there might be tens, hundreds, or over a thousand Quakers at a Yearly Meeting when it is in session. At a Yearly Meeting, there are usually times of worship and reflection, perhaps on a topical theme or something important to those gathered; decisions to be made, some routine business and some very significant, even life-changing; and social times, since the people gathered might never have met, or be old friends who only see each other at Yearly Meeting, or something in between.

Inside the big doll, there's usually a smaller doll – my image is going to start getting into trouble here, as this actually represents a whole set of meetings. Any individual Quaker only belongs to one of them, though! This layer is known as Monthly Meetings (they meet about once a month for business, or maybe every six weeks or ten times a year or something similar), or as Area Meetings (they cover a geographical area... but how big that is would be difficult to predict). In some places the Monthly Meeting looks after a whole set of smaller meetings, i.e. the next layer in the doll, while in other places these two are combined into just one layer. The items of business which need to be dealt with change too, but typical subjects handled at this level include membership (who formally belongs to the Quakers), money and property (like owning buildings), and community building (like running social and educational events).

As I already said, there might be another layer – a Local Meeting (it's local) or Preparative Meeting (it prepares for the monthly meeting) or possibly a worshipping group (it just meets for worship and does little if any decision-making). There can be a lot of confusion here because different Yearly Meetings have more or fewer levels, but this is probably the meeting you would find first if you went looking for some Quakers, if there are any at all near you. This is the meeting in which the regular worship is held, as described in my chapter on 'Why do Quakers worship in silence?'.

In these layers there might be all kinds of internal structures. Any meeting might have committees, working groups, regular activity groups, or similar. Most will have asked a group to take responsibility for the quality of worship and the spiritual development of people there. Most will ask a group to look out for people's more practical and social needs, whether that's first aid or a listening ear or a communal meal. There might be groups working on issues which are important to the meeting, studying something (often the Bible or Quaker thought, but many other things), or doing something practical together (often with the aim of helping others, or keeping the meeting house in good order). Bigger meetings will need people to work on the internal organisation – to keep paperwork up-to-date, to handle finances, to maintain communication within the community, to find people to do different kinds of work, and so on. It's usually healthy for these structures to be reviewed and changed from time to time, or the world changes around them and they get out of touch.

Right at the middle of the doll, there's an individual. This is the Quaker who attends the worship and belongs to the meeting and, ideally, participates in some of its activities, including the decision-making meetings. Inside the solid doll at the middle of a set of nesting dolls, there are all sorts of fascinating things – wood grain for traditional dolls, emotional and spiritual and intellectual life for people – but to write about all that would be a different book.

Working outwards again from the individual, we can think about how an idea or suggestion spreads through these networks. Suppose someone, let's call them Sam, feels strongly that God is asking them to take on a task and they want the community to support them – in Quaker jargon, this might be called 'acting under concern' and the support given is known as the community 'adopting the concern'. Sam would start by talking to people in their local meeting, perhaps informally first and then bringing the question to the nearest meeting for worship for business. 'Will you support me in this work?' The meeting prays, and might say no, or offer specific forms of support (money, time, people for Sam to talk it through with, etc.), or might both offer support and say that it needs to be shared more widely. In that case the meeting can forward it to the next layer. If the next meeting also says yes, the concern might get forwarded all the way to the Yearly Meeting to which Sam's meeting belongs.

In this way, almost all Quaker communities belong to networks of Quaker meetings, so they can offer and receive support, share ideas, and sometimes get together. Because the details vary so much by region, the best way to find out about how Quakers local to you sort this out is to find them or their website and ask. For example, here are five websites from Yearly Meetings which explain their ways of doing things:

- Australia: https://www.quakersaustralia.info/organisation
- Britain: http://www.quaker.org.uk/our-organisation/our-structures
- Ireland: https://quakers-in-ireland.ie/about-us/structure/
- New York: https://www.nyym.org/content/nyym-organization
- Philadelphia: https://www.pym.org/our-structure/

Why don't Quakers volunteer for roles within the Quaker community?

In order to ask this question, you need to know some basic things about the Quakers. First, you'd need to know that unprogrammed Quakers don't usually appoint paid pastors or anyone else who might be seen as a priest or minister for hire. Second, you'd need to know that although most Quaker meetings are run entirely or mainly by unpaid work, very few of the individuals doing that work volunteered.

In case you missed one of those, let me take a moment to talk about them in detail. First one first: many Quakers don't appoint paid ministers or pastors. Why not? Early Quakers were rebelling against a church which they saw as full of highly educated, greedy, controlling people – people who claimed to be Christians but didn't teach true Christianity, who were in the Church for the status and the money but not interested in serving God or helping people develop spirituality. If you're sure your paid church leader isn't like that, then this isn't a critique of your church. If the suggestion upsets you, maybe you have suspicions. Many paid faith workers today aren't in it for the money – their church, or synagogue, or mosque, or other organisation pays them just enough to live on, or provides housing rather than some of the money, or pays them part-time, but it's by no means a get-rich-quick scheme. On the other hand, I can also think of some who seem to be making money and buying private jets or other status symbols, so perhaps there are places where this criticism is valid. There's also a side to the Quaker critique which isn't about the money, but rather about lack of inspiration. If you're expected to preach a sermon every week, for example, is it going to be genuinely led by God every week? Or are you sometimes going to speak routinely, habitually, or from your own ideas rather than what God really wants you to say? Early

Quakers thought they knew a lot of preachers who fell into this trap. They wanted to get out of these expectations and have open worship in which whoever was led to speak, would speak, and that meant not appointing anyone in advance.

Now I'll move on to the second bit: most of the Quakers doing unpaid community work didn't volunteer for that specific piece of work. What you can volunteer for varies by meeting – I've worshipped at places where you can volunteer for the tea and coffee rota, and places where someone else judges whether it's appropriate to put you on that rota. (They usually listen if you ask to be removed.) Anything more serious than that usually has to go through what's called a 'nominations committee'. (Names may vary regionally.) The nominations committee is a group of people who are specifically tasked with finding people to take on roles in the community: for example, a Quaker meeting might ask its nominations committee to find a new member for the pastoral care team. Using the same Quaker business method by which almost everything in a Quaker meeting is decided – see 'Why do Quakers make decisions in worship?' for details – the nominations committee reviews possible names, decides who to approach, and when someone has agreed to take on the role, forwards that person's name to the meeting for worship for business, who appoint them.

When this works well, it's a system which can match up people with roles they find satisfying, in teams that work well together, in ways which can enhance people's spiritual growth. Sometimes the obvious thing for someone to do isn't really where their gifts are best used, and the things you would volunteer for may not be the things you really need to be doing. For example, I know someone whose professional training was in accountancy, but who didn't find any spiritual growth in being a treasurer – but was much happier as a clerk for the meeting for worship for business. I also know that left to myself, I'd opt for things which are easy for me and visible, because I like being seen and acknowledged; but the behind-the-scenes ordinary work and the things I find challenging are just as important. Roles I've thought would be boring or too hard for me have often proved educational. Many nominations systems also build in the idea that any individual only serves in a role for a limited time, perhaps three or six years. When this is done, people often find that it brings a freshness to the jobs. The work is shared around the community, there are new learning opportunities, and in a different role you get a different perspective on the whole life of the community. Sometimes it gives you things nobody but God could have known you needed.

That said, there are always ways in which it can go wrong. People's personal desires can overtake their sense of what God wants, and so steps are often taken to prevent the nominations committee becoming a clique or keeping hold of too much power – for example, nominations committees don't nominate their own replacements. Instead, people to serve on the nominating committee are found by a separate nominating group often created just for that one task. Similarly, nominating committees often decide to take steps to make sure the people they approach aren't completely unwilling or unsuitable. In a small community, they might speak individually to everyone they think might be able to contribute by some form of service, while in a larger community they might send out a form and ask everyone to comment on their experience and interests. Some nominations processes also use a kind of reference, asking someone else who knows the person well for comments – ideally with the permission of both the person who might be nominated and the person giving the reference!

For people who are new to this system, it can be very confusing. Compared with direct volunteering, it might seem to lack simplicity or honesty – especially when expressing interest in a specific role in the community might make sure you are never asked to serve in that way (or might get you asked, different nominating committees take this different ways). Sometimes nominations committees ask more people than they need names to take back to the meeting for worship for business, but the difference between being sounded out – 'would you be interested in this?' – and being asked to serve – 'we'd like you to do this, are you willing?' – isn't always clear. People can be deeply hurt by these and other misunderstandings, poor communication, or genuine cases of being excluded. Compared with an election (where you might get voted down but at least you have some clear numbers on how badly you lost), being nominated or not can seem lacking in transparency. There are lots of ways in which these things can be addressed without losing the core benefits of the system, but meetings sometimes rely on telling people to 'trust the discernment' of the committee.

Any volunteer-based system needs people to volunteer. The nominations system needs people to accept nomination, and it can run into trouble if there aren't enough people willing to serve or the jobs all seem too difficult. Sometimes at this point meetings revisit their first assumption. For example, it can be hard to find a community member who's willing to be a treasurer, but it's possible to make the job much easier by paying someone to do the book-keeping. For other roles, they might need to revisit the job description. They might split up the role differently, as when they appoint three co-clerks instead of a clerk and an assistant clerk. They might share it very widely: rather than asking a committee of four people to provide pastoral care to the whole meeting, they might ask everyone in the meeting to provide pastoral care to one or two others. Alternatively, they might look at the piece of work and decide it's not needed any more. Perhaps God called for that to be done for a while, but not any more, and that's why nobody feels led to accept a nomination for it. Accepting this and 'laying down' a project is a Quaker tradition which sometimes feels right.

To find out more about this process, you could:

- read Roy Stephenson's book *Freeing the Spirit: Nominations in the Society of Friends in Theory and Practice* (2009, William Sessions Ltd): https://bookshop.quaker.org.uk/Freeing-the-Spirit_1850723923
- look at the free leaflet, 'Principles and Testimonies: Nominations' produced by Britain Yearly Meeting (find the download link under 'Quaker business' on this page: http://www.quaker.org.uk/resources/free-resources/outreach-materials)
- read this blog post from Bob Tajima of Santa Monica Friends Meeting about Nominating Committees: https://www.fgcquaker.org/cloud/santa-monica-friends-meeting/resources/nominating-committee

Why are Quakers so political?

Some years ago, I opened my front door to some evangelists from another church. We exchanged the usual opening moves – they offered me a copy of the *Watchtower*, I offered to trade it for some Quaker literature, they refused – and as a follow-up they started asking me more about Quakerism. My meeting had recently been doing some research into our local conscientious objectors, people who refused to fight during the First World War when legal provision for them to opt out of the draft on moral grounds was thin, so I started there. It made good common ground, since Jehovah's Witnesses are also conscientious objectors.

Then they asked about other forms of participation in national life. Do Quakers vote? Yes, we do. The Jehovah's Witnesses are surprised – they don't vote, they told me, because they are ruled by God, not by human governments. Me too, I said, but God works through human hands, so we need to be involved in governments here and now in order to try and build heaven on earth. They asked whether it had ever worked, and I said yes. I said that I thought the introduction of same-sex marriage was a sign that our British government at the time was moving closer towards treating everyone equally, as God would want. I knew before I said it that the Jehovah's Witnesses couldn't possibly agree, and sure enough the conversation ended soon after.

The question they raised is a good one. Why do Quakers vote? Actually, Quakers don't just vote – individual Quakers stand for election, groups of Quakers campaign on many issues, and generally participate actively in the democratic life of the nations in which they live. How does that sit with refusing to participate in the military? How does it fit with the Quaker way of making decisions and their rejection of voting for internal use? Does it mean that Quakers as a group are aligned with a political party?

I'll start with that last one and work backwards. No, Quakers are not aligned with a specific political party – individual Quakers may be members of any political party. There can be trends. Quaker business people were often associated with *laissez faire* economics and hence with economically liberal parties. Some other Quakers have been attracted to socialism and the labour movement, perhaps especially because of its emphasis on equality. Today, some might have any of these views, or others – a more recent trend is for Quakers to be concerned about environmental issues and active in political parties with that specific focus. Any of these things can make it look like Quakers favour one political party (especially if you ask three Quakers who are all friends, and they all agree), but overall it isn't possible to say that Quakers are affiliated with any given party.

That doesn't answer the question about why Quakers are even joining political parties in the first place. Shouldn't they be sticking to religious stuff or doing charitable work without getting into politics? Well, for Quakers these things aren't separable. Quakers make religious claims which have political implications – it might not always be clear exactly what those implications are, but claims like 'going to war is always wrong' or 'everyone is equal' move quickly from their religious origins to the political sphere. Then there's the challenge of working out how to prevent war: A strong social justice movement to share resources and make war unnecessary? Fight this enemy to prevent it happening again? Refuse to participate and hope everyone else will, too? Abolish national boundaries so there's nothing to fight over? Build strong links between communities so it's impossible to see anyone as the 'enemy' and kill them? Something else? All of the above? I think it's at that moment, when you need practice and policies, where Quakers have most of their disagreements. The theory – putting faith into practice not just in private but also in public life – is widely agreed.

As I have already said, this theory can be expressed in lots of different ways. Some Quakers focus on 'speaking truth to power', telling it like it is to politicians and policy-makers. That can include voting, since voting is one of the means people are given in a democracy by which to speak up. It can include non-violent direct action, like blocking the route to an arms base or breaking in and trying to put the weapons out of use. It can include lots of campaigning tactics, from starting or signing petitions to going on marches or writing letters. Because of the emphasis in liberal Quakerism on personal experience, this often goes with a move to try and listen to the voices of those most directly affected – who may or may not already be within the community. Hearing from gay, lesbian, and bisexual Quakers has been important in Yearly Meetings which have decided to support same-sex marriage. Exchanging letters with prisoners who are on death row, who may have had no previous contact with Quakerism, is both a way of campaigning against the death penalty by treating those people as equals but also a way of learning about the conditions and the laws involved. In examples like this, the principles which underlie the Quaker way of making decisions – here, listening to as many different perspectives as possible in order to try and get a rounded picture – are put into practice even in settings where the rest of the Quaker business method won't be used.

Quakers, then, are active in politics as a way of living out their faith in the world, not as a distraction from it. Although there is an argument that living in a nation protected by a military force makes you indebted to that force – and so obliged to help it when called upon to do so – Quakers don't generally accept this argument. (In any given war, some Quakers have accepted this argument, and some have accepted that although most wars are wrong, this particular one is necessary. Pacifism is a Quaker tradition, but there are many ways to look at the moral problems war presents.) Instead of seeing themselves as indebted, Quakers tend to look for what they can offer to the nation. That might be practical – some people who refuse military service will act in an ambulance unit, for example, or others focus on relief work. It might be political – just holding a strict pacifist line in public debate might open up space for others to move in that direction, even a little way. It might be both – because Quakers have a clear 'big picture' of heaven on earth, or the Divine Commonwealth, they tend to relate practical charity work, like helping destitute refugees, to specific political campaigns, like opposing unjust laws for asylum seekers.

Quakers are political, then, because of the faith commitments they have. They have many understandings of those faith commitments and they interpret the political implications of their beliefs differently, but liberal Quaker faith today is completely compatible with and may even lead to political action.

To find out more about this, you could explore:

- John Lampen's book, *Quaker Roots and Branches* (2018, John Hunt/Christian Alternative Press): https://www.johnhuntpublishing.com/christianalternative-books/our-books/quaker-roots-branches
- QuakerSpeak's video, 'Why Do Quakers Care About Politics?': http://quakerspeak.com/why-do-quakers-care-about-politics/
- an article on Quakers and politics from Quakers in the World: http://www.quakersintheworld.org/quakers-in-action/89/-Politics

Conclusion: what will Quakers be like in the future?

Throughout this book, I've tried to give a brief glimpse of the diversity of Quakers today, and some of the ways in which they have changed over time. For almost every question I've addressed, the answers vary around the world – across and within different Quaker traditions, and would have been different if I'd written this book a hundred or even fifty years ago. So, what might happen next? What will Quakers be like in the future?

The only thing I can say with complete confidence is that Quakers will change. Quakers, like every other faith community I've ever studied or heard about, have changed in the past and are changing now, so this a safe thing to expect.

I'm willing to go a little further, though. Here are three predictions, ranging from the minor to the dramatic, which I think are moderately likely (although, in a traditional Quaker phrase, I also consider it possible that I may be mistaken).

Quakers will continue to become more aware of themselves as a complex, global community.

Some Quaker groups will split over disagreements, probably about the nature of God and what is acceptable among people, while other Quaker groups tackle the same issues but manage to keep a sense of unity.

Quaker meetings and churches will remain lively communities with something important to offer the world – predictions of the death of religion are premature.

I make all of these predictions in the context of a much bigger situation: the global climate problem. This needs urgent action – action which some Quaker groups are already involved in, and which Quakers often have the skills to help with. Living simply often means living more sustainably, so Quakers have practical things to offer. Speaking truth to power has often involved taking direct action or finding successful ways to campaign, so Quakers have political skills to offer. And climate breakdown is tied up with questions of justice, the fair distribution of resources, and empowering neglected groups to speak, so Quaker methods and commitment to equality have something to offer, too.

Some Quakers have always had a strong international awareness. Quakers throughout history have travelled, whether to visit other Quaker groups, to spread the Quaker message, for business or family reasons, or to go to centres of political power. However, the rise of global communication – especially the Internet – enables many more small, direct connections to be made. International connections aren't new to Quakerism (Quakerism spread outside Britain within a few years of its founding, and got together the Friends World Committee for Consultation in 1937), but the shape of communication has changed. Individual Quakers at home no longer have to hear reports from those who have travelled, but are increasingly able to turn on a phone or open a laptop and speak personally to Quakers from other countries and other traditions. They don't even have to set out to do that: if you search for Quakers on a social media site, you will accidently find Quakers who are from a range of yearly meetings and have different ways of being Quaker. This increases awareness. Together with more formal means of connection, it creates space to share ideas and perhaps work together on joint projects. In 2012 a world conference of Quakers held in Kenya issued the Kabarak Call for Peace and Ecojustice, which historians might one day regard as a starting point for a global Quaker campaign on climate change. (You can read it online at http://www.fwcc.world/call.pdf)

In this book I already described some of the ways in which Quakers have developed in different directions. Quakers worldwide have already split over issues around theology, ways of working and worshipping, and sexuality. Those questions don't go away, and new ones are asked. For example, people might leave Quaker communities – and/or create new Quaker communities – because of disagreements about issues such as whether Quakers need to believe in an external deity, the treatment of transgender people, or at what stage it's time to protest not only a particular politician's behaviour or a specific policy, but the whole system of government and economics. I know what answers I want my Quaker community to reach (on the three issues I mentioned: nontheist Quakers are Quakers, trans and nonbinary people are and should be recognised as the gender they say they are, and we should protest the system whenever it is causing harm, just in case you were wondering). I also know – and perhaps this is a typically Quaker thing to say – that the process by which we reach those answers is important. In describing how a community reaches a decision in unity, sometimes we use the metaphor of a journey. We don't all have to travel at the same speed or by the same route, and sometimes it will look like we're going in different directions, but eventually the community arrives at a destination together. I trust that we will eventually arrive, because that's part of my faith in our way of seeking direction from the Divine Mystery. I also confidently predict that it will take a while.

Quakers have a lot to give, and I don't think the community is dying out. Some people have made dire predictions, usually based on the trend in numbers in some yearly meetings – but there are three other things to take into account. One is the worldwide picture; liberal Quakers, like many other churches in the countries where liberal Quakers are the most common kind of Quakers, are shrinking, but liberal Quakerism isn't the whole story. A second is the fact that even where Quaker numbers are falling, they aren't falling as fast as numbers in other churches. A third is that Quakerism can change, and might change in a way which leads to stabilisation or growth. If Quakers keep speaking out boldly, and people see that the Quaker way has something to offer, Quaker communities might grow. If Quakers keep practising our way of worshipping and making decisions, and people see that the Quaker way brings spiritual and practical benefits, Quaker communities might grow. If I'm right that Quakers have something real to offer to people struggling to make the changes which are needed in a time of climate breakdown, Quaker communities might be transformed by the process of offering to everyone those practical, political, and spiritual skills.

I hope that this book has helped to explain why Quakers do things the way they do. For everything I've said here, I've tried to point to sources of further information because it would be impossible to sum up all of Quakerism in a single book. In the end, though, I also want to point you to another source. Instead of reading anything else, or watching a video or something, you could also consult the Inward Light.

Quakers know from experience that when we settle down and listen, we have access to something which gives us new perspectives, opens doors, sows seeds, gives rest, moves us to action, and enables us to do what love requires of us. Whatever Quakers do in future, it will come from this holy source, which is available to everyone, everywhere, at all times.

More questions?

A book like this can't answer every question. For more information about Quakers, you could contact:

- Friends World Committee for Consultation: http://fwcc.world/
- Friends General Conference: https://www.fgcquaker.org/
- Friends United Meeting: https://www.friendsunitedmeeting.org/
- Quakers in Britain: https://quaker.org.uk/

Or many other specific Quaker groups – put Quaker plus your location into a search engine.

You are also welcome to contact me directly:

- email rhiannon.grant@woodbrooke.org.uk
- write to Woodbrooke, 1046 Bristol Road, Birmingham, B29 6LJ
- look at the Woodbrooke website: https://www.woodbrooke.org.uk/
- find me on Twitter at @bookgeekrelg
- find me on Facebook as Rhiannon Grant

Also in this series

Quaker Roots and Branches
John Lampen

Quaker Roots and Branches explores what Quakers call their
'testimonies' – the interaction of inspiration, faith and action to
bring change in the world. It looks at Quaker concerns around
the sustainability of the planet, peace and war, punishment,
and music and the arts in the past and today. It stresses the
continuity of their witness over three hundred and sixty-five
years as well as their openness to change and development.

Telling the Truth about God
Rhiannon Grant

Telling the truth about God without excluding anyone is a
challenge to the Quaker community. Drawing on the author's
academic research into Quaker uses of religious language and
her teaching to Quaker and academic groups, Rhiannon Grant
aims to make accessible some key theological and philosophical
insights. She explains that Quakers might sound vague but are
actually making clear and creative theological claims.

What Do Quakers Believe?
Geoffrey Durham

Geoffrey Durham answers the crucial question 'What do
Quakers believe?' clearly, straightforwardly and without
jargon. In the process he introduces a unique religious group
whose impact and influence in the world is far greater than
their numbers suggest. *What Do Quakers Believe?* is a friendly,
direct and accessible toe-in-the-water book for readers who
have often wondered who these Quakers are, but have never
quite found out.

CHRISTIAN ALTERNATIVE
BOOKS

THE NEW OPEN SPACES

Throughout the two thousand years of Christian tradition there
have been, and still are, groups and individuals that exist in
the margins and upon the edge of faith. But in Christianity's
contrapuntal history it has often been these outcasts and
pioneers that have forged contemporary orthodoxy out
of former radicalism as belief evolves to engage with and
encompass the ever-changing social and scientific realities. Real
faith lies not in the comfortable certainties of the Orthodox,
but somewhere in a half-glimpsed hinterland on the dirt track
to Emmaus, where the Death of God meets the Resurrection,
where the supernatural Christ meets the historical Jesus,
and where the revolution liberates both the oppressed and
the oppressors.

Welcome to Christian Alternative... a space at the edge where
the light shines through.
If you have enjoyed this book, why not tell other readers by
posting a review on your preferred book site.

Recent bestsellers from Christian Alternative are:

Bread Not Stones
The Autobiography of An Eventful Life
Una Kroll
The spiritual autobiography of a truly remarkable woman
and a history of the struggle for ordination in the Church of
England.
Paperback: 978-1-78279-804-0 ebook: 978-1-78279-805-7

The Quaker Way

A Rediscovery

Rex Ambler

Although fairly well known, Quakerism is not well understood. The purpose of this book is to explain how Quakerism works as a spiritual practice.

Paperback: 978-1-78099-657-8 ebook: 978-1-78099-658-5

Blue Sky God

The Evolution of Science and Christianity

Don MacGregor

Quantum consciousness, morphic fields and blue-sky thinking about God and Jesus the Christ.

Paperback: 978-1-84694-937-1 ebook: 978-1-84694-938-8

Celtic Wheel of the Year

Tess Ward

An original and inspiring selection of prayers combining Christian and Celtic Pagan traditions, and interweaving their calendars into a single pattern of prayer for every morning and night of the year.

Paperback: 978-1-90504-795-6

Christian Atheist

Belonging without Believing

Brian Mountford

Christian Atheists don't believe in God but miss him: especially the transcendent beauty of his music, language, ethics, and community.

Paperback: 978-1-84694-439-0 ebook: 978-1-84694-929-6

Compassion Or Apocalypse?
A Comprehensible Guide to the Thoughts of René Girard
James Warren
How René Girard changes the way we think about God and the
Bible, and its relevance for our apocalypse-threatened world.
Paperback: 978-1-78279-073-0 ebook: 978-1-78279-072-3

Diary Of A Gay Priest
The Tightrope Walker
Rev. Dr. Malcolm Johnson
Full of anecdotes and amusing stories, but the Church is still a
dangerous place for a gay priest.
Paperback: 978-1-78279-002-0 ebook: 978-1-78099-999-9

Do You Need God?
Exploring Different Paths to Spirituality Even For Atheists
Rory J.Q. Barnes
An unbiased guide to the building blocks of spiritual belief.
Paperback: 978-1-78279-380-9 ebook: 978-1-78279-379-3

Readers of ebooks can buy or view any of these bestsellers by
clicking on the live link in the title. Most titles are published
in paperback and as an ebook. Paperbacks are available in
traditional bookshops. Both print and ebook formats are
available online.

Find more titles and sign up to our readers' newsletter at
http://www.johnhuntpublishing.com/christianity
Follow us on Facebook at
https://www.facebook.com/ChristianAlternative